I'M GOING TO TEXAS
YO VOY A TEJAS

by
Mary Dodson Wade

translated by
Guadalupe C. Quintanilla

illustrated by
Virginia Marsh Roeder

COLOPHON HOUSE   HOUSTON, TEXAS

*For Keri's —
Yeah, Texas!
where his Grandad lives —
Mary Wade*

For all those who think Texas
is nothing but cowboys.
---M.D.W.

For my four wonderful girls
and Richard.
---V.M.R.

ACKNOWLEDGMENT: A special thanks to Pat Anthony for encouragement and to Betty Peña, Adanevia Martinez, and Myrthala Rodriguez, along with all those wonderful people in El Paso, for perceptive reading, comments, and clarification. "Don't Mess with Texas" logo used by permission of the Texas Department of Transportation.

Cataloging-in-Publication Data
Wade, Mary Dodson
  I'm going to Texas/Yo voy a Tejas/by Mary Dodson Wade;
trans. by Guadalupe C. Quintanilla; illus. by Virginia Marsh Roeder.
  p. cm.
Summary: Going to Texas involves more than just being a cowboy.
Interesting places beckon adventurous travellers.
ISBN 1-882539-17-6
ISBN 1-882539-18-4 (pbk)
[1. Texas—Fiction. 2. Texas—Description and Travel. 3. Spanish Language
Materials—Bilingual. 4. Stories in rhyme.] I. Roeder, Virginia Marsh, ill.
II. Quintanilla, Guadalupe C., tr. III. Title.
PZ8.3W12Im 1995
917.64
[E]

Copyright © 1995 by Mary Dodson Wade
All rights reserved
Printed in the United States of America
Published by Colophon House

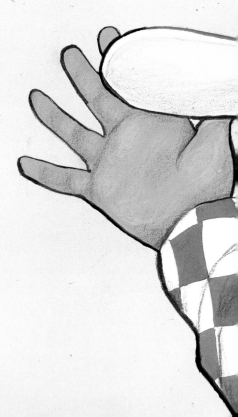

"I'm going to Texas.
I'll wear a big hat."

*Yo voy a Tejas.
Usaré un sombrero grande.*

"Texas has cowboys,
but it's more than that."

Tejas tiene vaqueros,
pero tiene mucho más.

Texas has many ranches, but the largest one, King Ranch where Santa Gertrudis cattle were developed, spreads over several counties in south Texas. The town of Albany calls itself home of white-faced Hereford cattle. Cowboys show their skills at rodeos in Mesquite, Stamford, and Dalhart.

Tejas tiene muchos ranchos, pero el más grande, el King Ranch (el Rancho Rey) donde se desarollaron las vacas Santa Gertrudis, cubre varios condados al sur de Texas. El pueblito de Albany se conoce como el lugar de nacimiento de las vacas Hereford, que tienen caras blancas. Los vaqueros demuestran sus talentos en los rodeos de Mesquite, Stamford y Dalhart.

Fort Worth was once called Cowtown. Visitors to the George Ranch Historical Park near Richmond get a close-up view of life from 1820 to 1930, including cowboys. But ... the most famous Cowboys in Texas play football in a stadium in Irving, near Dallas.

A Fort Worth se le llegó a llamar el Pueblo de la Vaca. Los visitantes al parque histórico George Ranch (el Rancho Jorge) cerca de Richmond pueden observar de cerca la vida típica desde 1820 hasta 1930, incluyendo vaqueros. Pero los Vaqueros más famosos juegan football en un estadio en Irving cerca de Dallas.

"I'll put on my chaps
and ride through the cactus."

Me pondré mis chaperreras,
y pasearé entre los nopales.

The Piney Woods of East Texas is covered with trees. Sandy beaches bring flocks of sunlovers to Galveston and Padre Island. Tall buildings rise out of the blackland prairie in Dallas, and Houston's Ship Channel has miles of oil refineries.

El Piney Woods of East Texas (el Bosque de Pinos en el oriente de Tejas) esta cubierto de árboles. Lindas playas atraen a mucha gente a Galveston y Padre Island. En Dallas, grandes edificios surgen por la llanura negra, y Houston's Ship Channel (el Canal de Barcos de Houston) tiene millas de refinadoras de aceite.

"In some parts of Texas that's not the practice."

En ciertas partes de Tejas, esto no se hace.

Austin, the capital, is part of the Hill Country, famous for its wildflowers. El Paso bumps up against the mountains, while Amarillo sits on the flat, wheat-growing High Plains. Orange trees grow in the Valley, near Brownsville.

Austin, la capital, es parte de Hill Country (el area de colinas de Tejas), que es famosa por sus flores silvestres. El Paso llega a las montañas y Amarillo se encuentra en el llano donde se siembra trigo. Naranjas crecen en el Valle cerca de Brownsville.

Dancers swirl at Fiesta Texas in San Antonio. Theme parks like Six Flags over Texas near Dallas and Six Flags AstroWorld in Houston have stage shows along with thrill rides.

Los bailarines jiran en Fiesta Texas en San Antonio. Parques como Six Flags over Texas (Seis Banderas sobre Tejas) cerca de Dallas y Six Flags AstroWorld en Houston tienen espectáculos y paseos emocionantes.

"I'll pull on my boots
and dance the Cotton Eyed Joe."

*Me pondré mis botas,
y bailaré el Cotton-Eyed Joe.*

"You can dance in Texas
or watch a big show."

*Puedes bailar en Tejas,
o ver un gran espectáculo.*

Famous performers entertain fans at annual rodeo and livestock shows in Fort Worth and Houston. Outdoor theaters recreate Texas history each summer on Galveston Island, in Palo Duro Canyon, and at El Paso.

Famosos artistas divierten a las personas en los rodeos anuales y en las exposiciones de ganado en Fort Worth y en Houston. La historia de Tejas se recrea en teatros al aire libre cada verano en la Isla de Galveston, en Cañon Palo Duro y en El Paso.

"I'll jump on a mustang
and race over the hills."

*Brincaré sobre un mustang,
y correré sobre los cerros.*

Mustangs used to run wild across Texas. Now huge bronze ones splash across the plaza at Los Colinas in Irving.

Los mustangs antes corrían salvajes a traves de Tejas. Hoy en dia, estatuas de bronce chapotean a traves del agua en la plaza de Las Colinas en Irving.

"Texas has horses
and many more thrills."

*Tejas tiene muchos caballos,
y muchas cosas divertidas.*

In Brenham members of the Monastery of St. Clare raise miniature horses no bigger than a large dog. Tiny Round Top has wonderful old houses and a ranch with miniature donkeys.

En Brenham miembros del monasterio Sta. Clara crián caballitos pequeños no más altos que un perro grande. El pueblito de Round Top tiene maravillosas casas antiguas y un rancho con burros de miniatura.

"I'll lasso a steer
and take a wild ride."

*Lazaré un novillo,
y tomaré un paseo alocado.*

"Texas has cows
and other animals beside."

*Tejas tiene vacas
y muchos otros animales.*

San Antonio, Brownsville, Dallas, and Houston have outstanding zoos, but there are many wild animals such as deer, squirrels, and, of course, armadillos. Rare whooping cranes return each winter to Aransas Natural Wildlife Refuge. American bald eagles are spotted on the Vanishing Texas River Cruise out of Burnet.

San Antonio, Brownsville, Dallas y Houston tienen zoológicos estupendos pero también hay muchos animales salvajes como venados, ardillas y armadillos. Gruellas raras regresan cada invierno al Aransas Natural Wildlife Refuge (Refugio Natural de Aransas). Aguilas calvas americanas se han visto en el Vanishing Texas River Cruise (paseo por el rio tejano) en Burnet.

Lubbock and Snyder have prairie dog towns in the city. Alligators abound at McFaddin Wildlife Refuge near Port Arthur. There are even rattlesnake roundups every year in Sweetwater and Big Spring.

Las ciudades de Lubbock y Snyder tienen pueblitos de tuzas. Los lagartos abundan en McFaddin Wildlife Refuge (Refugio de Animales Salvajes de McFaddin). Hasta hay un gran evento para accorralar víboras de cascabel en Sweetwater y Big Spring cada año.

"I'll go looking for Indians.
They'll be all around."

Iré a buscar indios.
Están en todos lados.

Alabama-Coushatta Indians live in east Texas near Livingston and the Tigua Indians near El Paso. All the other tribes are gone.

La tribu Alabama-Coushatta vive en el oriente de Tejas cerca de Livingston y los Indios Tiguas viven cerca de El Paso. Ya no se encuentran otras tribus.

"Texas has Indians,
but they're not easily found."

Tejas tiene indios,
pero no se encuentran tan fácil.

Texas was named for the Tejas Indians, and their Stone Age home near Alto has been excavated. Indian pictographs, some over 1000 years old, decorate ledges at Hueco Tank Park near El Paso, in Seminole Canyon near Del Rio, and at Paint Rock.

A Texas se le nombró por los indios Tejas, cuyos hogares prehistóricos cerca de Alto se han excavado. Dibujos indios, algunos de más de 1,000 años, decoran los muros en el parque Hueco Tank cerca de El Paso, el Cañon Seminole cerca de Del Rio, y en Paint Rock.

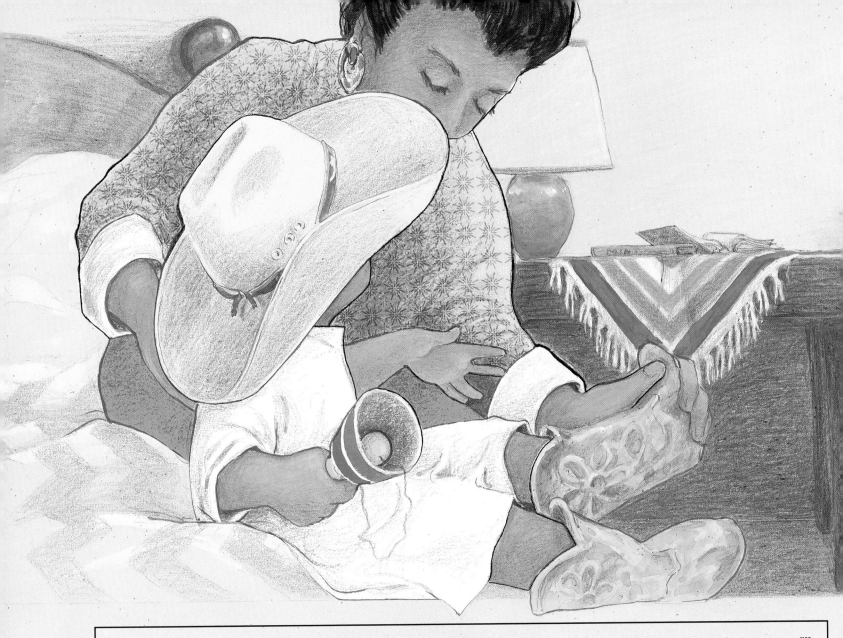

In San Marcos glass bottom boats give a view of fish and underwater plants. Sea creatures, both tiny and monstrous, fill the Texas State Aquarium in Corpus Christi. Vacationers splash down the Schlitterbahn in New Braunfels, float down the Guadalupe River on innertubes, or surf the white sands at Monahans.

En San Marcos lanchas con fondos de vidrio proporcionan un lindo panorama de los peces y las plantas bajo el agua. Criaturas del mar, pequeñas y monstruosas, llenan el Texas State Aquarium (el acuario del estado) en Corpus Christi. Los turistas salpican en el Schlitterbahn en New Braunfels, flotan en el río Guadalupe en tubos de llanta o esquian sobre las arenas blancas de Monahans.

"The cook will serve beans.
I'll taste a few."

El cocinero servirá frijoles.
Yo los probaré.

"There are other things in Texas
besides eating to do."

Hay muchas cosas que hacer en Tejas,
además de comer.

Dinosaur tracks reveal prehistoric Texas inhabitants at Hondo, Glen Rose, and Sattler, but dinosaurs were not the tiny creatures that created the great Texas oil fields. Museums with derricks and displays explain the process in Kilgore and Midland. Visitors ride the steam train from Rusk to Palestine, climb Enchanted Rock's bald surface near Fredericksburg, and explore the Caverns of Sonora.

Huellas de dinosaurios revelan los habitantes prehistóricos de Tejas en Hondo, Glen Rose y Sattler, pero no fueron los dinosaurios las criaturas que crearon los grandes depósitos de aceite. Museos en Kilgore y Midland revelan el proceso de bombear aceite. Los turistas se pasean en el ferrocaril de vapor de Rusk a Palestine, suben la lisa Enchanted Rock y exploran las Cavernas de Sonora.

"I'll sit by the campfire
and play my guitar."

*Me sentaré cerca del fuego,
y tocaré mi guitarra.*

"There are more things in Texas
than you've dreamed by far."

*Hay muchas cosas en Tejas
más de las que puedes imaginar.*

In San Antonio, hushed visitors walk through the Alamo and see a picture of the real David Crockett. Shamu leaps from the water at Sea World, and boats glide along the Riverwalk. Circus fans marvel at the Hertzberg Circus Collection. In Dallas, Big Tex greets visitors to the State Fair each fall. The Frontiers of Flight Museum at Love Field gives the history of aviation.

En San Antonio los turistas caminan con reverencia por el Alamo y ven un cuadro de David Crockett. Shamu brinca del agua en Sea World y las lanchas se deslizan atraves del rió. Los fanáticos del circo se maravillan de la colección del circo "Hertzburg". En Dallas, Big Tex da la bienvenida a los visitantes a la Feria del Estado en otoño. El museo Frontiers of Flight (Frontera de Aviación) en Love Field de la historia de la aviación.

Near Huntsville is a huge statue of Sam Houston. In the city of Houston, sports fans cheer in the Astrodome. An inspection boat offers a free ride down the ship channel. San Jacinto monument, not far away, honors Texas independence and presents a magnificent view from its top. But the most popular attraction is the Johnson Space Center in Clear Lake where visitors see what it is like to be an astronaut.

Cerca de Huntsville hay una estatua gigante de Sam Houston. En la cuidad de Houston, los fanáticos deportistas aplauden en el Astrodome. El barco de inspección ofrece paseos gratis por el canal. El monumento de San Jacinto, no muy lejos de Houston, honra la independencia de Tejas y tiene una vista maravillosa desde lo alto. Pero la atracción más popular es el Johnson Space Center de Clear Lake donde visitantes pueden ver lo que es ser un astronauta.

"I'll sleep on my saddle
under stars big and bright."

*Me dormiré sobre mi silla de montar,
bajo las estrellas grandes y brillantes.*

"You'll have great fun in Texas.
And now...good night!"

*Vas a divertirte mucho en Tejas.
¡Buenas noches!*

AROUND TEXAS

ALBANY - 110 miles west of Fort Worth on US Highway 180.

AMARILLO - on Interstate 40 and US Highway 87 in the Texas Panhandle.

ARLINGTON - 15 miles west of Dallas on Interstates 20 and 30, location of Six Flags over Texas.

AUSTIN - state capital; located 80 miles northeast of San Antonio on Interstate 35.

BIG SPRING - on Interstate 20 about half way between Dallas and El Paso.

BRENHAM - 60 miles northwest of Houston on US Highway 290 [Don't miss the Bluebell ice cream.]

BROWNSVILLE - southern tip of Texas, on border with Mexico, on US Highway 77.

BURNET - 55 miles northwest of Austin on US Highway 281 at Texas 29. Reservations needed, (512) 756-6986.

CLEAR LAKE - southeast area of Houston, 30 miles from center of the city, off Interstate 45.

CORPUS CHRISTI - 140 miles southeast of San Antonio on Gulf of Mexico, Interstate 37 and US Highway 77; Texas State Aquarium located on North Shoreline Drive off US Highway 181.

DALHART - 75 miles northwest of Amarillo on US Highway 87 at US Highway 54.

DALLAS - Interstates 35E and 45 at Interstates 20 and 30; zoo located at 612 E. Clarendon; State Fair Park located in east Dallas on Grand Avenue and 2nd Street; Love Field located in northwest Dallas off Loop 12; Six Flags over Texas is located in Arlington halfway between Dallas and Fort Worth off Interstate 30.

DEL RIO - 150 miles west of San Antonio, near border with Mexico, at US highways 90 and 277.

EL PASO - extreme west tip of Texas, on Interstate 10 at the Rio Grande River; Tigua Indian Reservation (Ysleta del Sur Pueblo) on Old Pueblo Road off Interstate 10 east, exit Loop 375 (Avenue of the Americas).

ENCHANTED ROCK STATE PARK - 18 miles north of Fredericksburg on R.M. 965.

FORT WORTH - Interstate 35W at Interstates 20 and 30; Stockyards Historic Area on north side along Exchange Avenue.

FREDERICKSBURG - 70 miles west of Austin on US Highway 290 at US Highway 87.

GALVESTON - 60 miles southeast of Houston on Interstate 45.

GLEN ROSE - 45 miles southwest of Fort Worth on Texas 144 off US Highway 67.

HONDO - 30 miles west of San Antonio on US Highway 90.

HOUSTON - Interstate 10 at Interstate 45; ship channel is Buffalo Bayou east of the center of the city; Astrodomain (site of Livestock Show and Rodeo as well as sporting events) and Astroworld located on South Loop 610; NASA is in Clear Lake half way between Houston and Galveston; Hermann Park Zoo is east of downtown off Kirby Drive.

HUECO TANKS STATE PARK - 30 miles east of El Paso on County Road 2775, off US highways 62/180.

HUNTSVILLE - 90 miles north of Houston on Interstate 45; Sam Houston statue visible from interstate.

IRVING - Texas (Dallas Cowboys) Stadium located at Loop 12 and Texas 183; Los Colinas located a few miles north of Texas Stadium on Texas 114

JOHNSON SPACE CENTER (NASA) - located in Clear Lake section of Houston.

KILGORE - East Texas Oil Museum on US Highway 259 at Ross Street.

KING RANCH - located in Nueces, Kenedy, Kleberg and Willacy counties in extreme south Texas ; entrance west of Kingsville off Texas 141.

LIVINGSTON - 90 miles northeast of Houston on US Highway 59; Alabama-Coushatta Indian Reservation 15 miles east of Livingston on US Highway 190.

LUBBOCK - 120 miles south of Amarillo; Prairie Dog Town in Mackenzie State Park off Interstate 27; Ranching Heritage Center next to Texas Tech. University off Loop 289.

MESQUITE - east of Dallas on Loop 635 just south of US Highway 80

MIDLAND - 335 miles west of Dallas on Interstate 20; Permian Basin Petroleum Museum located 1500 West Interstate 20.

MONAHANS - 250 miles east of El Paso on Interstate 20; Sandhills State Park is five miles east of city on Interstate 20.

NEW BRAUNFELS - 25 miles northeast of San Antonio on Interstate 35.

PAINT ROCK - 30 miles east of San Angelo on US Highway 83; Indian pictograph tours leave from office in town.

PALESTINE - 115 miles southeast of Dallas at junction of US highways 79, 84, and 287.

PALO DURO CANYON STATE PARK - 30 miles southeast of Amarillo, off Interstate 27 on Texas 217.

PORT ARTHUR - 20 miles south of Interstate 10 in Beaumont, on Louisiana border; McFaddin Wildlife Refuge office on south on Shell Oil Company road off Texas 87.

RICHMOND - 20 miles southwest of Houston on US Highway 90; George Ranch Historical Park is 8 miles east of city on Texas 762.

ROUND TOP - half way between Houston and Austin, south of US Highway 290 on Texas 237.

RUSK - 30 miles east of Palestine on US Highway 69 at US Highway 84.

SAN ANTONIO - Interstate 10 at Interstates 35 and 37; Alamo located downtown on Commerce Street; Riverwalk located below street level downtown; zoo located at 3903 N. St. Mary's; Hertzberg Circus Collection located 210 West Market; Sea World located 15 miles northwest of center of city, off Texas 151.

SAN JACINTO BATTLEGROUND STATE HISTORIC SITE - 20 miles east of Houston off Texas 225.

SAN MARCOS - 40 miles northeast of San Antonio on Interstate 35; Aquarena Springs on Spring Lake.

SATTLER - 35 miles northeast of San Antonio, west of Interstate 35; Dinosaur Flats are 2 miles southwest on F.M. 2673.

SIX FLAGS OVER TEXAS - in Arlington on Interstate 30 at Texas 360.

SNYDER - 200 miles west of Fort Worth on US Highway 180; prairie dogs in city park; white buffalo statue on square.

SONORA - 170 miles northwest of San Antonio; caverns are west of city, 7 miles south of Interstate 10 on RM 1989.

STAMFORD - 150 miles west of Fort Worth on US Highway 277 and Texas 6.

SWEETWATER - 195 miles west of Fort Worth on Interstate 20.

Text set in 18 pt. Tymes Roman type
with titles in 32 pt. Harem
Printed on 80# Mead Moistrite Matte paper
Mixed media art
Printing and binding by Walsworth

Author Mary Dodson Wade and her husband have lived in Houston for nearly twenty years. A former librarian, she usually writes biographies, but this book is her way of letting everyone know that Texas is more than cowboys. It also reflects her love of travel — in Texas and out.

Illustrator Virginia Marsh Roeder studied graphic design at Pratt Institute in New York and worked as a successful commercial illustrator. She moved to Texas when she married and taught art in Houston, where she and her husband have lived for a number of years. This is her first children's book.

Translator Guadalupe C. Quintanilla, born in Mexico, came to the United States as a teenager but was not motivated to learn English until her three children were placed in slow-learner classes. By her determination, she learned English and so did they — two are lawyers and one a medical doctor. Dr. Quintanilla is Assistant Vice-President for Academic Affairs at the University of Houston.